DOT-TO-DOT
MACHINES

Karen Bryant-Mole

Illustrated By Graham Round

Edited by Jenny Tyler

Factory machines

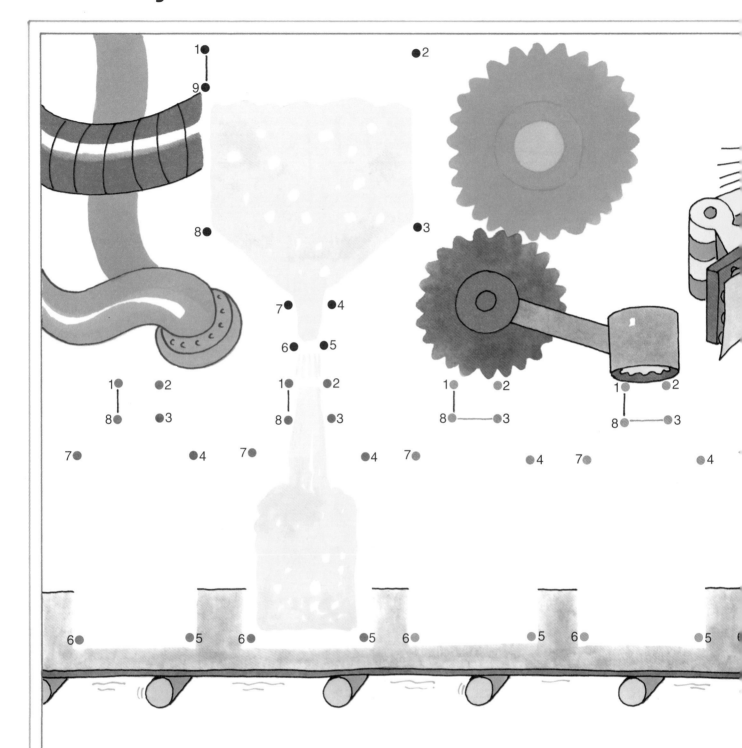

Cat and mouse are working in the lemonade factory.

- Join the red, brown, orange, pink, yellow and blue dots to see the bottles on the conveyor belt.

- What is the machine doing to the bottles?

1 2 3 4 5 6 7 8 9 10 11 12 13 14 15 16 17 18 19 20 21 22 23 24 25

- Join the black dots to see the part of the machine that fills the bottles with lemonade. You can fill in the bottles with a yellow pencil.

- What is mouse doing? Join the green dots to find out.

Racing machines

- Join the red and green dots to find two very fast machines.
- Join the yellow dots to see something that goes slowly.

26 27 28 29 30 31 32 33 34 35 36 37 38 39 40 41 42 43 44 45 46 47 48 49 50

Building machines

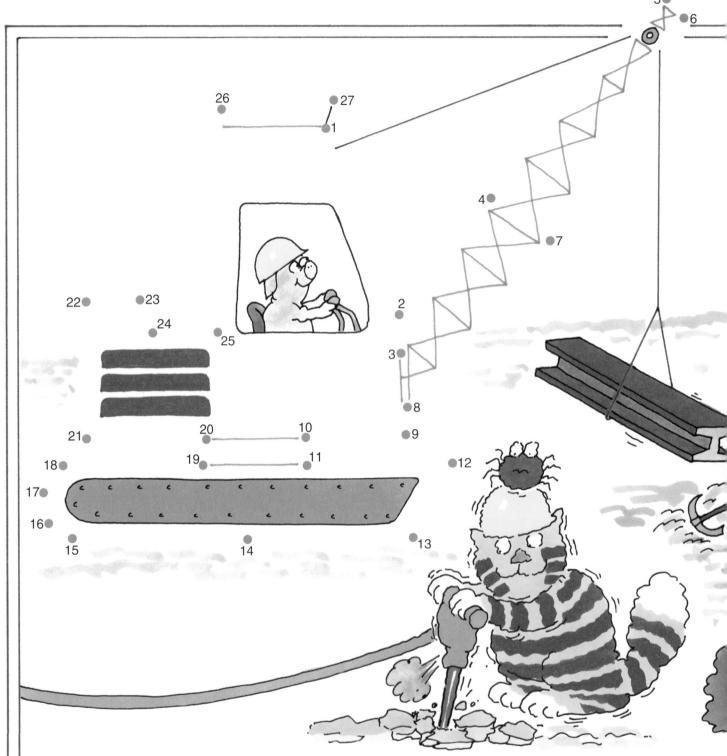

The animals are working hard on the building site.

- Join the green dots to see the machine pig is using to lift a heavy girder. What is this machine called?

- What can you see if you join the blue dots?

1 2 3 4 5 6 7 8 9 10 11 12 13 14 15 16 17 18 19 20 21 22 23 24 25

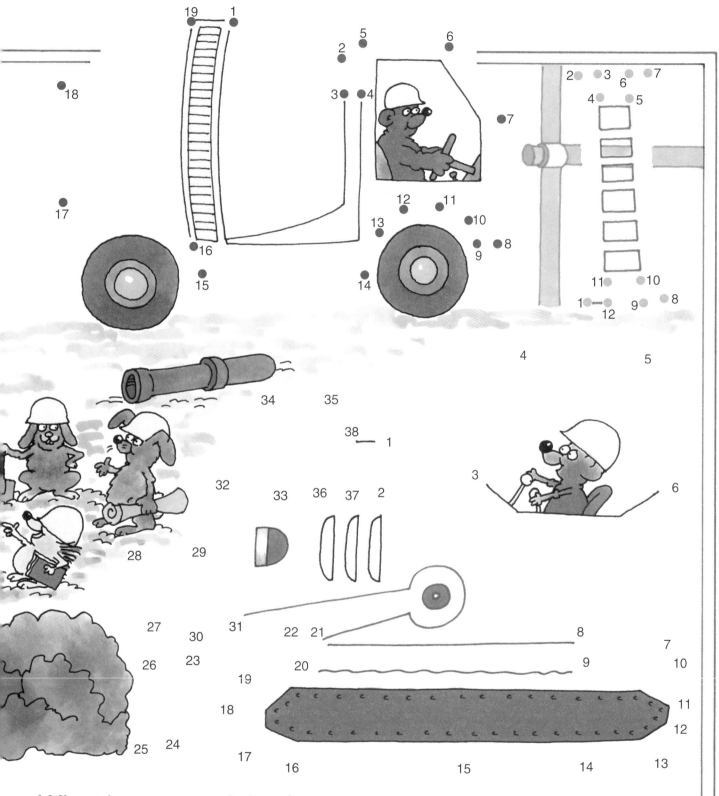

- What is mouse doing?
  Join the yellow dots to find out.

- Join the red dots.
  Do you know what this machine is called?

Machines in the air

The animals are going flying.

• Join the yellow dots to find out what cat is flying in.

- Join the red dots and green dots. What can you see?
- One of these machines is a plane and the other is a glider. Planes have engines. Gliders have very long wings and no engines. Which is mouse flying?

Road machines

- What is bear driving? Join the green dots to find out.
- Join the yellow and orange dots to find out what frog is driving.

1 2 3 4 5 6 7 8 9 10 11 12 13 14 15 16 17 18 19 20 21 22 23 24 25

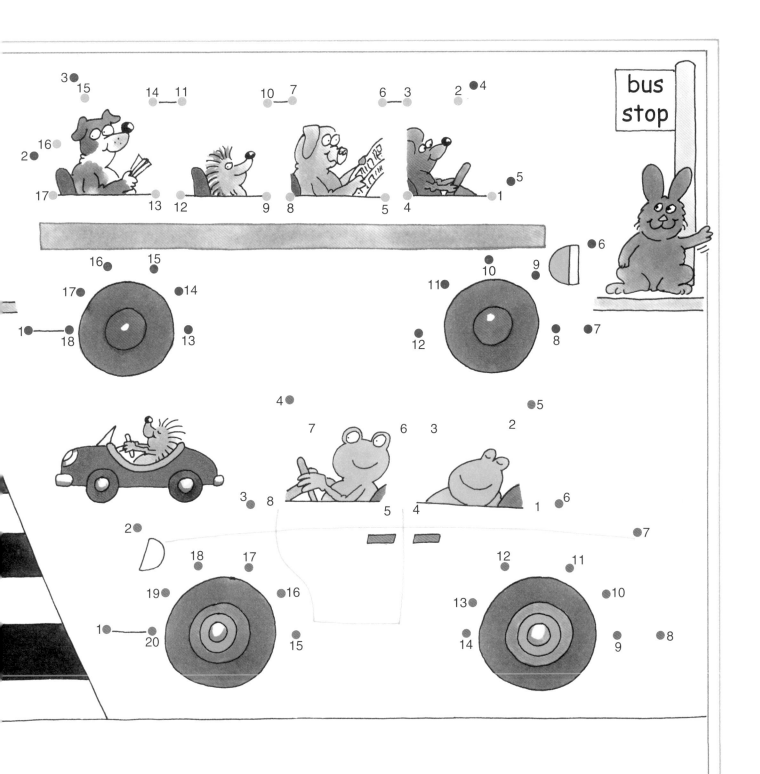

- Join the red dots to see what mouse is driving.
- Join the blue dots to help his passengers see out.

Machines at sea

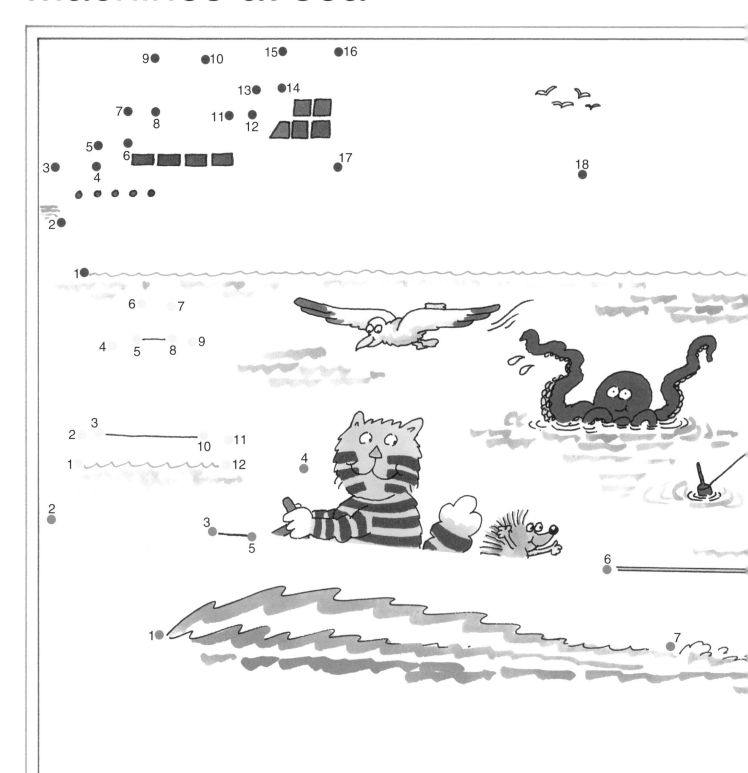

- Can you find an oil tanker, a fishing boat, a speedboat and a passenger ship in this picture?
- Join the red, blue, green and orange dots to see them all.

1 2 3 4 5 6 7 8 9 10 11 12 13 14 15 16 17 18 19 20 21 22 23 24 25

- Join the yellow dots. What can you see?
  (It is a buoy which warns ships of dangerous rocks under the water.)

- Who is water skiing?

Steam machine

Can you guess what the animals are doing now?

- Cat is driving a steam engine. Join the green dots to see what is looks like.

- The engine has a very hot coal fire in it. This heats water to make steam and the steam makes the engine go.

1 2 3 4 5 6 7 8 9 10 11 12 13 14 15 16 17 18 19 20 21 22 23 24 25

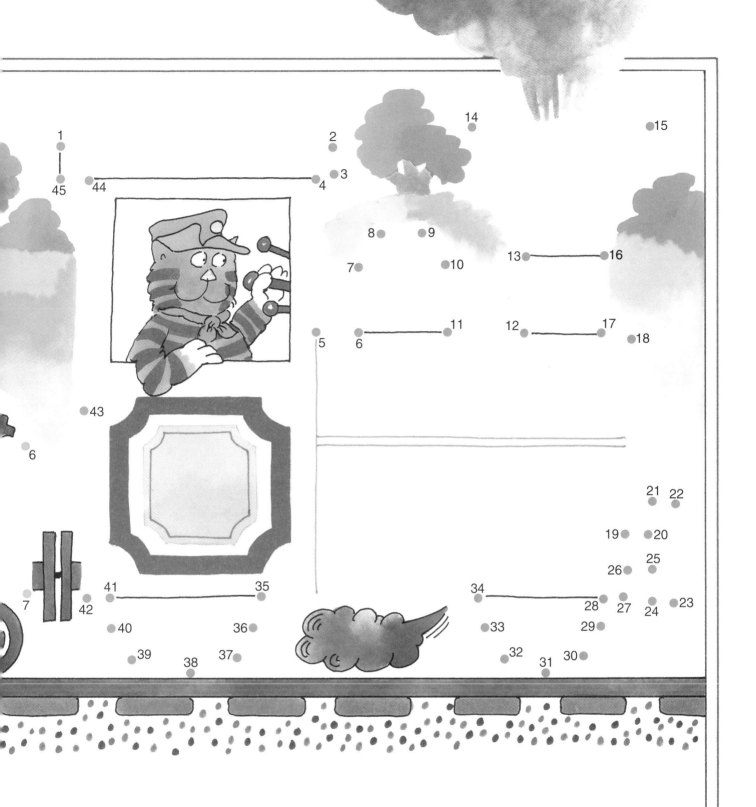

- Join the blue dots to see where the coal is stored. Whose job is it to put the coal on the fire?

- Join the red and yellow dots to find out what the passengers are sitting in.

26 27 28 29 30 31 32 33 34 35 36 37 38 39 40 41 42 43 44 45 46 47 48 49 50

Space machines

Cat and mouse have landed on a strange planet.

- Join the red dots to see cat's spacesuit.
- Join the green dots and you will see his landing craft.

1 2 3 4 5 6 7 8 9 10 11 12 13 14 15 16 17 18 19 20 21 22 23 24 25

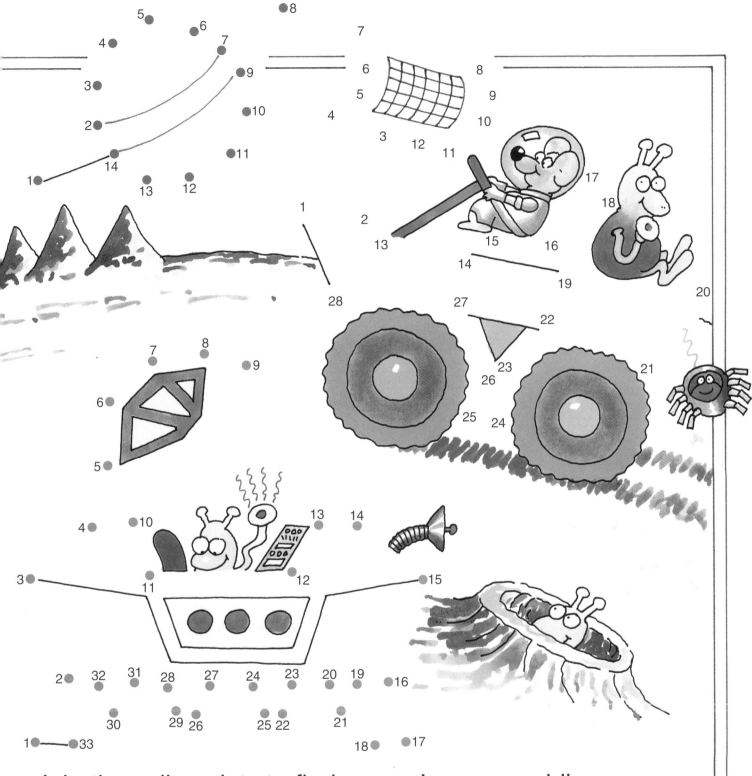

- Join the yellow dots to find mouse's spacemobile. Can you see its radar?

- Where is hedgehog? Join the blue dots to find out.

- What can you see when you join the orange dots?

26 27 28 29 30 31 32 33 34 35 36 37 38 39 40 41 42 43 44 45 46 47 48 49 50

Emergency machines

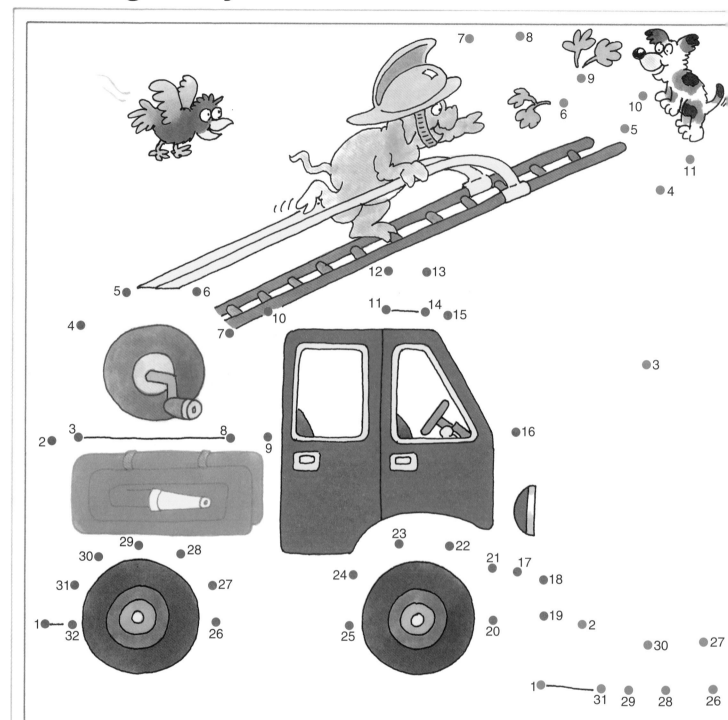

Dog is very worried.

- Join the green dots to see where her puppy is.
- Who is coming to the rescue?

1 2 3 4 5 6 7 8 9 10 11 12 13 14 15 16 17 18 19 20 21 22 23 24 25

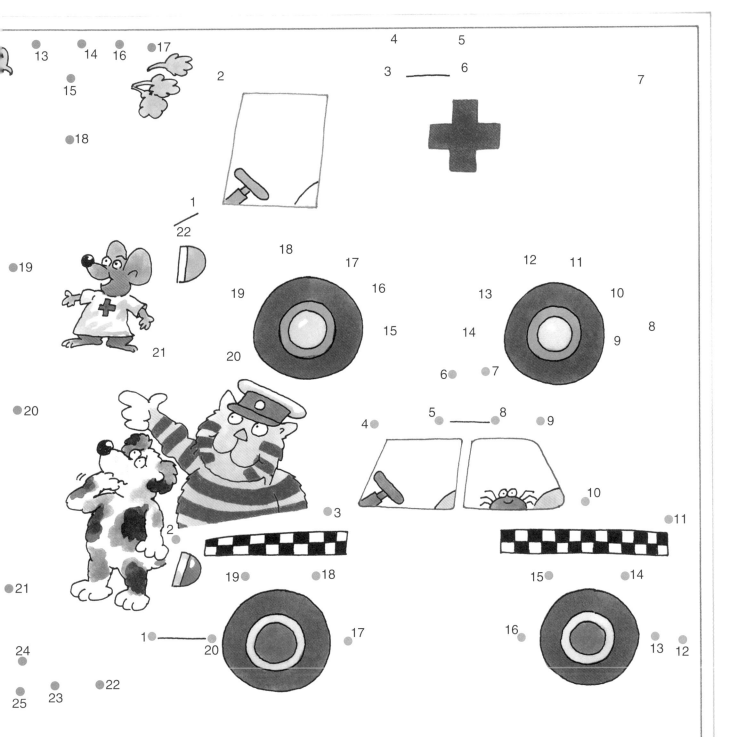

- Join the red dots to find out if you were right.
- Join the yellow and blue dots to see who else has arrived to help.
- Can you spot spider?

Fairground machines

Cat is buying a ticket to go on the merry-go-round.

- What animals are there to ride on?
  Join the red, blue and yellow dots to find out.

1 2 3 4 5 6 7 8 9 10 11 12 13 14 15 16 17 18 19 20 21 22 23 24 25

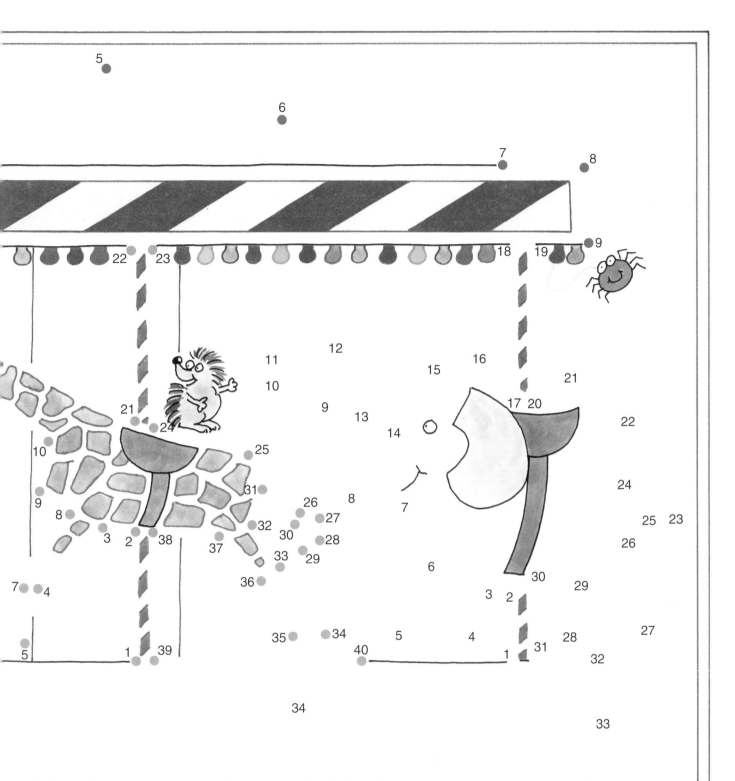

- Join the orange dots to finish the merry-go-round.
- What other fairground machine can you see when you join the green dots?

Toy machines

The animals are testing toys in the toy shop.

- Cat hasd found a remote-controlled toy. What is it?
  Join the orange dots and both sets of green dots to see.

1 2 3 4 5 6 7 8 9 10 11 12 13 14 15 16 17 18 19 20 21 22 23 24 25

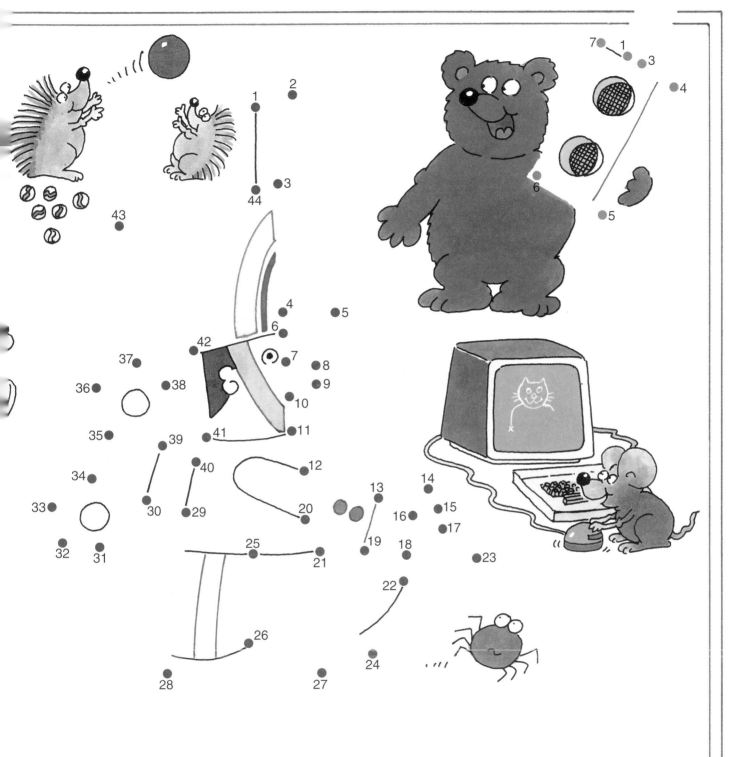

- Join the red dots. How does this toy work?
- What are pig and bear doing?
- Join the pink and blue dots to find out.

Home machines

Mouse is busy at home.

- Join the blue dots to see what he is doing.
- Vacuum cleaners need electricity to make them work. Join the green and red dots to find more electrical machines.